PROTECTIVE IMMEDIACY

PROTECTIVE IMMEDIACY

Rod Smith

ROOF BOOKS

NEW YORK

ISBN-13: 978-0-937804-78-0
ISBN-10: 0-937804-78-9
Library of Congress Card Catalog No. 99-61352

Book design & typography by Barbara Campbell
Cover design by Deborah Thomas
Cover photo: New York Public Library

Versions of these poems have appeared in *The Baffler, B City, Cathay, Explosive, The Germ, I Am A Child, The Impercipient, Lingo, New American Writing, Open 24 Hours, Philly Talks, Phoebe, Primary Writing, Tool: A Magazine*. Some of these poems appeared in the Potes & Poets limited edition *Protective Immediacy* (1998). *The Boy Poems* was published as a chapbook by Buck Downs Books in 1994. "A Grammar Manikin" appeared as a special feature in *Object#6*.

Roof Books are distributed by
Small Press Distribution
1341 Seventh Avenue
Berkeley, CA. 94710-1403
Phone orders: 800-869-7553
www.spdbooks.org

This book was made possible, in part, with public funds from the New York State Council on the Arts, a state agency.

NYSCA

Roof Books
are published by
Segue Foundation
300 Bowery
New York, NY 10012
seguefoundation.com

for Josh

Table of Contents

The Boy Poems

*Humor is a process. Depression
a useful first step.*
—Ian Scholes

George.

Mink skin
    is mission's
  abroad & upgrade & detrained
fission-gist,
        meanwhile
   "take you to the empty place
  in my
  fire engine"

     — the fake
     actual —

Use form 290666654B1A stroke & overprint dash.

    the actual
    flakes
    on the makeshift
    geniality

    of love

Rick.

Dice and then try
The character developed a sincere expression
"In life" as more motley arranged the room
recedes   Some attempt at singularity
They say grandiose about a bank and guaron tee
If I seems slightly distracted it's because
The birds lost again

Boris.

colliding & colliding

more than mixtures

more than access

treacle & comely

the social spores

goad & appease

mercurially incensed

smother domed

supper cones

Harold #2

Speaker: Agon means

that ache you can

really see, right?

non-speaker: in some

x, the gross national

awkward. Oh hell,

Speaker: "Prove it"—

non-speaker: Special lights

I blow then sip, brains

dumped over pumps, etc.

Speaker: Diet *across*

that; then what?

Woodward.

Javanese trailers inching

backward through the

hooch. Soon as it

reduxes we'll hop

on by. Zoner sinks

maudlin, marriage,

mercurial, moribund

just

eat   O,
          by the way,
this   radical theory will always
          be quickly institutionalized,
real   and real experience cannot but
          pass into spectacle.
loud   There is room for regret, but
          not for analysis.
     Please write your representative about
          these concerns.

Harold.

Supreme kook.

Void arrangement
qua mama clock—

> the videop
> soporifically
> redefined
> as mimicking
> pseudo-combinant
> spillage—

Viably zonk.

Visibly clunk.

Simon.

The implicit is
Arrival, approach
impasse— a hand issuing from a grasp—
These alternatives cannot be harmonized.

But harmony sucks anyway.

Larry.

Halls,
  reasons
    olfactory
yet certainly contrived.

    The vice *is*
    the victim. One time
without looking
    the barnyard needed
some sorta transfusion. One time

a dick like that was;

    Mince
    your
    words
    or
    mind
  your caricature—

note lip

at lease

no ease

(appease)

Lucifer.

Viaduct off-spring of a slinkie

salesperson—

> Divorce
> or
> acutely vivid—

> (welp)

> dyspeptic area code
> yet recombinatory, on ceremonial
> disturbed water stoop

Say the sound
&/or slay the swingline

> Some say need
> is a statutory explanation
> of the mobility
> of synchronicity.

> Most of them are guilty
> of democratic leanings.

Meredith.

Eeking like a sandled
strand of tree stands.

    More often

completely
        arterial in his
        variable
        fricasee
        intonation—

the circles

seep products
clearly designed
for accurate, moss washed
bunker toes.

Vector.

     Jones of a dimmer
on that mattress stand ain't it.

      Coca-commotion™

    all the attention
    it syrupy &
    in weather
    mode as of
    the and the

desirous padded sorcery.

not very.

Bert.

His cosmology major falls like a free compass
point through the breakthrough of all emotional
life. A puritan background psychically fused
with the interdemensional thought-form of Portland
to produce a cathode ray capable of power-crazed
crop circles— This is the heart of all living
systems— The workshop mode flows formatively
across the morphogenetic light-born attractor
at the focal point of time and reemerges as
the Diet Coke stain on Bert's disintegrating
mostly purple tie-dye. Once, during his annual
abberation, it appeared to sweep out an eclipse.

Mel.

The same in a lesser sense
In a scene similar to the former
In full course as if scattering
In a variant of a sign
& the equipoise which it suggests
A youthful figure hovers over raised hands
Another reading reverses this

Bailey.

Occupies the time between
this sleep & this sleep.

The formative mystery inherent
in America as objective act.

Die to the bygone or bleed
on a borrowed timecard. Geeze.

Dutch.

Fresh pea soup (above)
flavored with mint
leaves, apples and
sherry, then thickened
with cream

There are worse, much worse, things than this.

Some passages are crazy— they are the products of a
mind no longer master of its fantasies, no longer
able to segregate fantasy from fact;

Small wonder then that one did not want
to let go of all this, that one opposed in every
conceivable manner a theory which involved for
him who accepted it the right and the challenge
of a hitherto unknown now undreamed-of
freedom of thought and elevation of mind.

Edmond.

His genius at least includes
ceilings. A journey wouldn't not
see the miniscule ethic as gradation
of food movement. Seek
monetary garnishes. Dr. Kissinger
shouted. He looked panicked.
"Are these copies yours?"
he asked.

Arthur.

> The fuse aggravates
> the atypical, yet alone there
> with some ink
> eye
> detonation—
> > industrious, incapable
>
> choreography in the twinite chamber

The Buddha.

    At Multiples, Inc., in New York, he produced *Star Quarters* (1971), a four-panel Plexiglass mirror with a brightly colored zodiacal whimsy silkscreened across the surface. The place where we were, but in another room. I know many artists who exhibit only a fraction of what they do so as to keep a chosen image of their work in the public eye.

John Fitzgerald.

—if ever in fact traces of free labor did exist...

I sense no longer the sense of this life's sense.
But rather am secreted by initial conditions.
I'm unhappy here
it seems rather
ignorant, this country
we agree we agree
the fates
they agree
the fumes
agree also it is
one of the things we like—
Dioramas vouch-safe
quasi-indigenous
portals of light realization.
we believe we believe
the ache
decides for itself
and the fortunate
have found everything already here
the bloodstream
in the growth on a headline
All this at the cost
of religion itself, 'Power'
and 'accident' are but
names for the causal chains...
that absence or
Demographic Questionnaire
it perturbs the crustaceans after all
you're wrong about clarity
I'd rather just sit
and watch the game

On the American Forces
Radio Network severance
of regained glossolalia
What's that little plan
you live in?
the failure, the inherent
'unnatural'
ask & you shall ask
crack this?
crack who?
Look up
on the lip
of the fool
are formal constraints
for fools. Freud
enjoyed the variable
refrain of the meritorious
surf & slipped on his
tile-colored tunic. The rushes
had shown him
that residual dystopic
impediments lay among the
legally blind objects
in the least of our
collections. But I
don't know what happened
to what happened. We lock
our keys in our surrealism.
—it is not thought that needs—
The dawn fills
the naked
& coughing
takes the true
tympany out the tongue
of the crystal teeth. A
jaundiced secretive

sergeant-like wind
soaps awake the rickety
temple— it
is all one
tomb,
bureaucracy, the caulked
occasion of us cradling
& carving & not crazed &
for most of the day
The great
enemy of clear language
is insincerity. It is not
easy, in the biography under
review, given the power of the
US propaganga system,
foisting more than a fair
share of the ritual indecency
on a flip diagnosis
of the savage beauty
we surround.
Forever isn't everlasting.
Tomb this dream of same.
They doom the lettuce
an appliance deserves…
If anything is excellent
or praiseworthy—
think about such
things. Time is money.
Thank you for your time.

Aaron.

    This morning we found ourselves covered with snow that had fallen during the night. If a lion could talk, we would not understand him. Dear father, what do you want to think? This part of Ohio smells like cheap lunchmeat. We ran out of hill I need a hill behind me it helps. This morning we found ourselves covered with snow that had fallen during the night.

The Classics

The Responsibility of Intellectuals

The sun is not gutted
or out on tour. The back-slap
of facticity is lost
on the F Train or else
available only
in outer space. The people
of Hanover, where they
make Utz, are genuine
with regard to their enthusiasms.
The essential writings
see them & say their adventure.
& yet, somehow unassailed,
is absolutely nothing.
The barber's concerns meld
or mesh with the cosmetologist's.
They are free.
The word pusillanimous
enters a conversation there, in Hanover,
& does not return. It has
gone home. Judgment
regarding this is not
worth a Knicks ticket.
If you place everything
you own in Hanover
it will disappear.

The Sublime Object of Ideology

A Nestea before the sex show
& a full length sofa bed
to teach the Cantos from—
this represents the temporal
hidden within the temporal.
The grapes though expensive
are "unimpaled."
Liquidity of the mischief,
a moist tint
Catalonia
love song on a breeze I
Do not feel
the high Titanic clockwork
when I touch her
or do I? Book of Life,
a new translation,
please. Pretty please.

The American Evasion of Philosophy

I'm dialing in & I don't want
to say it but
"your in-joke or mine"
comes to mind just as the machine's
signal beeps — it's
kind of custardy
...bonded and
capriciously acerbic
(we're talking *beyond* any "unsired" synchronous here)
but about Pepsi
I'd just like to know
& don't — it's a good deal —
sincerity's cotton belt
or Philly's new brew
How she then rethinks me
makes me
buy more wastepaper, american
waste paper, genuine
american
wastepaper
only as a symbolizing esthetic gesture
but still
wastepaper
like a sunbeam

The Prison Notebooks

they keep calling it "flour"
when the gunshops require
user-assistance
but nothing is toll-free
it goes by too quick
the profound is what is
secret

The Body in Pain

as opposed to what?

surreptitious & senile song-pus
zounds in the aquaint-port's temperate
Nile of metonomy-projection

the body of nubs takes it's muss to us

celibate   infinity

The Work of Art in the Age of Mechanical Reproduction

two airplanes meet
and fall in love.

reason-buzz
decides—

& is not true

& is not this right.
I am a turnip.

Fuff.

if it all went up in smoke
all perception would be by smell

"you don't trust many people
 & the ones you do trust leave"

a poem is a fracas
with a poem is a stew

sorry about the reference to Oz

sorry about all this matter

Write Like Soap

We're tired.

Fire the create crate soled.

                    The life to get top

ought to leak decease;

There's no trap, only subtle cushion
gathers sanction.
sanctions trust,
turns up

The date

(or torque) of that which there
on our said to it, would accumulate.

ditch the grand
task adjusts us
juggling a tune who's
nude flourish
masks a fluted
noose.

the woodpecker looks for dead trees, we

must then seek repose, explicitly

made of clay— *you* into *Space*

of inner-form hopefully
rice-bag as if listening

But they are not creative.
"brightly off the belly of a blimp"

is heard always from a distance…

allowing fancy to play with all the thought of pleasures
(The other model is also much discussed, I know) but only

to prohibit it, *baso continuo*—

      I resolved to spend a night.

colophonic talk

(and it escapes)

fairy dust (which is secular

(which from passion

inseparable subsidizes the socially

undertaken loaf's

freewill (my O)

Spokes them totally (which is not inept &

"has a yen for Ben" &

in its nature conditions

the rotten-toothed medullars'

conglomerate lucidity

The infinite redigitation plays tub tourniquet on the love-concern suit.
Like I like italian food I don't like. Licks inside schism factory:
walled wood doubt: Walled arc of the rote circuit waste:
menace tense, motor flow, apt earnest holding—

        The refill regroups — inker topple they is wooping
with a work up a whipped if dubbed in up a footstool reading
fluff.

menage a trois twine ± emoted donor

Couldn't we fill it with sand.

Coarse angel or coarse
right of fine

unsneaky
in its pusillanimous
exoskeleton

the shapes tent-force

linguiform
if co-decorous
apparatus for
or of
the turnstile axle
in the forsep of refuse:

cones
strike
the
sunstroke

prismatic
incarcerate abstinence

                              a slip

Gone as toward

& sit up upset voice—

unencumbered & overly
earthen,

                              the juice
                              in the jot,

        don't paraphrase—

            axe of context axe

            they or them or Amoco
            turn it off
            (a thin film)
            at the curbscrew
            ruler corked

The cycle.

feverish perpetuator
in the caucasian crayon box—

minister impy
riding the
gunker to the
fallow perspective—

divining the meek absinthe / soothe
about ink—

                Tea-ache-goaded
                neck-mini
                flotsam amidst kinky
         & purposive
         architectonic geyser—

They keep eeking out
enough about some Perfunctory
goggles   enough about some
ionized lecturers'
agate gunk

Forty times icicle

devious—   forty-four times
defunct

comeuppance askew
in the cradle of the
Night-owl
evading museumification

snap—

                        if an art ends in a Nissan...

The razor.
The nide oboe sides:

between the black nightshade
of the bittersweet morals
is certified
anchor come &
secret asynchronous
requiescat foam

legality's

jump-cut accompaniment

a cordoning skull & act
a light-perceiving piece of furniture

the mask ace
in the moot lesion

a total
recessed

cultural chunk derby

a strap that passes through
a restatement stagger

wander signature

circumpolar animus
& rural dean a dumb

back-lit abrasion

spasmodic center.

dust pulse.

spasmodic domes.

its its purposely
placement
up-sent (ing…
or
forks
up-sent inging)…

you can be nearly impossible

placement
of form inker
(desk virus)
& the canned loam of language
like I like timed licorice

IN THE FOLDER
motet a
coriander
constituent

That common workplace left its impression on our work

nome a duc...   appearance colluded/

the real compl—   or in tha graey a commonsense aqua

Rooted real, impairisoned, too tooled to extract invasion almost
our other maquette, more this sooning we operate closely a
kind of marinated froth where mean things activast carnal and.

                                        , a mar
                          on the soaked stone tooth

"generous"   that bee   that tomb that tune

Flare petals punt barbecue rep coc wicked marsh ought end.
For months the rising tactility. Fresh lanes of legs broom
from most to most. Suppose a side severs. Fill to it without
acting into more carriage return. Weed cosmogeny. Reckless
affect learns toil from year to date product code summary. Wier
to date, lest to fur, move to. Implode "we" —— form of tangerine,
The Era, "it's"

$$to = + , c \ omes \quad shift \ c, \ \#s? \qquad for \ x^3$$

The foam, the lashing business of

the foam my love. Were it twere pleased

lead. Chapter heading & fled Edges, mast

plops kite by tie

Almost inc.   The rule of mall   More first get

   sap of mare

glided by on way back for almost =

how does it happen. purged of all intellectual sediment

Buns
of
Philadelphia

import mortar plantiniridium
akin to so
seed oyster
liniment cap-a-pie

                              (licks inside

won't subside. Mazes,

furiously significant, type

a person out of

adjusted circus belief.

                    Just that

                              negotiable,

preposterous, pride & how

long it can talk, take it.

the simple persistent

List is
       of tilted   merit

                Durable access
depends on definite existence, George.
More of us like calling tomorrow

a way for— listing proximity as contribution.
red

             perception, the rude
copulent

              act as tho a problem's there

sight a
waiting for
turnipo

A Grammar Manikin

my bee beheld egghead star demon stuff like usual

Then came the punch line
more viscous than they said it was
In the words of Sir Arthur Stanley Eddington (title it)
ascot mock
ticko tock
gone quay machine
of nickle of kin
of Seth
the sequential
needle on the stet
singing
or indecipherable mainframe canine tv-shirt
that's an aside
& so,
Flamey, just remember
truth serum tastes
just like chicken with
cheeze wiz
I wish
the multi-patricianal
bludgeon icker
weren't so
more flan papa.

& feel nonetheless
a cold
cyclic difficult kitsch
done lucid on the
bank's brink dictates
deep stuff—

we fold
& in so doing
are retold
via the fictive commode
of the multinational toad.

a loaded gesture that lets assonance underscore dissonance is
a form of order within the identifiable classical Western nuclear
potatoes. <u>Roast Potatoes</u>
the pivot upon which
trans-informs enormous conceptual paste

The world would be a much better place if we all had
a well-articulated theory of implosion.

schmierkase schmo

schmoose

schmooze

schmuck

Schnabel

<u>jewels and binoculars</u>
<u>hang from the head of the mule</u>

Botany Bay it
by
hy-genie
generative grampa graduation
cluck cluck

what we haven't constructed
in space is praised by kissing

—tonal autogamy
(as opposed to total sodomy)—

do you like my "lyric thrust" better than his
          pocket veto
I'm calm
and pluri-detailed desuetude
Part 4:
          Desuetude Precontract

a record having allotted loan or overhanging sciatic spill
Breathe deeply and know that you are attuning your spleen chakra

"your footnotes are too violent"

but at what point did she say to herself
I wanna be a wonk

or is it febrile

does
as Aquitaine
dreams
as gastro-rich

yr local Stop & Flop in a monastic context
"They're just too democratizing in their character."
especially when amplified by those counter-sorcerers called
in polite company
The Tantric Inter-American Flexibility Conference on Dramatic
Sensory Focus

I am I because my little knowledge knows me

1. It is a great annoyance to have so many wishes

    2. "less is less"

411 is a joke

  4. which catalyzed the moment known as language riding

     5. If, furthermore, you ask, "What is Buddha?"
It is like shouting your innocence while holding the loot

    5.1 She/he likes your mysterious contemporary visual
          poetry & proposes marriage

    5.121 There were camera bunkers still standing
           from the famous test

countless dark ineradicable expert musician attachments
ablating dimerous stereotypes
light all totaled
shakeable dedication
&* vanish
these
that is
worlds
they will.

the satisfied
probably have
many novels
and always
float in the air
thinking
freedom from confusion.
irremediably <u>foreign</u> and <u>strange</u> which is no
im-sign physically A-frame & came
in my fiction and flame to quake webs of light

I'm sorry we do not accept Pagans as payment

— *I said*   I'm sorry we do not accept Pagans as payment

to kill a demon marry the most common decorative motifs.

a shaft
the rooms share

                                                  follows the

                                       horizontal

                      novice in the middle envy

administrative ruins
is perched

                              painted origin

                   And nothing   softens on a steep

Function

square base

squat stupa

rebuilt flashlight

a frieze

of pillared

footpath

smallpox.

amminal or venomal

any applicable apotheosis here

clientele cliff clew-line
decoupage of thought-control
—we both felt a bit glum—
Revolutionary theory is now the sworn enemy of all
revolutionary theory— light you also
intangible intake endstops
that's what I say

nay, the transnational will

let us literally

work with metaphysical tools.

away from repetitive particulars in a Neo-Sensory epithetical
skin-treatment flood tide
The good grease goes back goes in goes down goes under
Description is not necessarily distinct domestic debriefing

    yes, in gathering information
    the inflatable environment
    saw fit on your thighs, palms up
what does that mean
butterlamp think   cuculiform solitude
                                      so soldierly

I'm sawed

This is tin

embracery (title it)
the signifier / signified metathetic
makes us imagine
making dysyopia all better must
amount to the medieval ability to reparagraph
—say it ain't so brittle—
but the sum tottle seems to ink us out
sheepish science dealing & important
—neither Spain nor Plain—
a health-related basic thing that people matter more than money
This includes setup troubleshooting
& could by evil means make a bran-new recidivism good-oh

new paragraph
all abt yoga
good afternoon
good behavior

There's a humming-bird-size hawkmoth up here eating reporters

Protective Immediacy

Poem Composed of A.G. & C.B. suggested by S.J. & beginning with a line from Duncan

Eros naked in foreknowledge

dreamt grandfather needed many loves

amidst the make-believe blackberries

when the garden that I could be

betrays a long charm settling:

trash of the mind
trash of the world
sliding and then arrested—
immaculate
blame to spike
breakfast and see a lifetime
in which ornate matter is dispersed like a bomb
— relentless— in my dark earplugs
— relentless, flowers and buildings,
Sunlit Forelorn Reprehending Seepage
. . . . as a voice in a vision that's vanished.

XCVII ("she knows who she is")

for what we are, swart passion
"amount" (the liaison debt)
    six & 1/2 to one, or the Having will acquire
SILVER as the need's I
    and just as false
    "and just as false"
as chide triangulated mist sinks me or me
                    (rivulet of competent
purse & grave, a gravity
relent in peace to stand bled
& strain. each out to false.
to turbulence. to time before
that codes grief cycle
    gist in the tones & riled re-wave
     says, and so is, and so the lowly
can be saved,
           but from
               purpose
      & turbulent, the taste
        is troubled,
& an accordance
abuts transcendence
       & crushes us, internal
for the thought doomed strong
      does not tense in it
       "we" are a crime
or foundations, effectively mist
felled before   current events
a crisp descent, not innocent
        the complacent bit's history
                 a cretinous
      aggregate, a young explorer, but the net

torque canned against the likes o

                                        that gaze

worn scrupulum's caste of ash
the torn internal
in the right honorable reticence
                    take it back
                    that
hitting head moment
June 9th, '68
            Cape Thing
                off the coast of Superficiality
snored in a cone — a brave deed
            you can drive around
                        a somehow made not nascent
        rent by shade
—"maybe partying will help"—
        but within love's coy tract
shave that soldered salve (ouch)
            is formed or is our failure or is
    a tongued environment's impetuous debility
they keep us locked up layers of non-sent slapping
            love in the purified finite
a gasping torqued thought-finish
on the effective mist
            this ludicrous business
this sadly ossified empty
                    final, injured, found waning
    an orchestrated probable praised by motion
it's circuit that again torn is thought they locked
        blazing in the blazing
say to it this form's shunt seed
say to it "closure"
as a clanged jack assays a coral cloud-document breath of
tazed intent
in the growth aglow

the bombed fundamental
      re-bombed futz of gut-us consumpt
& wayward   leaning on a star

Protective Immediacy

You're always suspicious
that you may not be doing
what you think you're doing.
Cigarette a letter to oneself
(again)
she writes "paw or paw"
on the large canvas &
never "sold out" their fetishization
of autonomy— the volcidestrians
are wiping the Natl. Capital Area
with fuckin candy rainbows
You're always suspicious
that you may not be doing
what you think you're doing.

actually she got quite a lot
for their fetishization of autonomy
tho nearly nothing for
sleeping crap
by Walter Benjamin
infinity seams
the body (between
space) decanters
the formal acuity
in a self-regarding rarity
K is for cathedral
& John is telling you
to help the Lizard tribe,
will you?

Things are not *OK*
Ismene, not several, & to drink
books in an unsurpassable
pariah-so-I-trash-it
story which is precisely
misled space possessed
& bled eyebath coupling &
nonrepresentational in the scare quote
salve in the cistern
of flamboyant earth-abundant
bursts
in the graving motion
as the upsurging
presence dies.

presence dies

in the lunge of trademark tradewind
"giving" — all night,
she is gone so
a cigarette tells
sleeping crap
of the unopened pack
of the latin word for cartoon
things among things
totally strange
the ritual preliminaries
the rages of attachment
bewilderment and evasion

in the scare quote salve
they're fixing the next
totally strange
illumined delusion
A beautiful ornament with us
extent, & Big Bouvon Fuller
has a blanket he uses to
carry conceptions of
ghosts— his face, a mandala
of a thousand star clusters
a Baby Monitor Music
of identity to soothe
conflict & nightmares inside
offerings of flame, & of speech

there's no storm before the calm
keeping the stopping still
        offering instead of living
& planted, Plato's ideas
dispute sharpness
        prefer Sappho
prefer [perfect] good [   ]
    [   ] iny
        vast surely day

But, Dr Williams
they die miserably,
anyway

& the light goes on on the
kneeling Ave Maria no sun
shining — come —
looking wood
hold off
so that we could meet
in my bag —
close I felt
it was content
even though I still didn't

history — you can read it —
you can snow —
Bernadette cupped it in her hands
a hole filled with cured place
<u>because & in response</u>
I read the manuscript
thinking about the fog
glass shook &
tell everything afraid beside the fruit
form
of a cross town bus
to happen to
police we have a strange stolen
love at the moment
to you w/ a poem some said nothing
was trembling
is like a popsicle
you can read drinking itself
to see it script
with no sharp edges
the last part always
falls off
on the damp pavement behind us
burning
the creative process
on yr clothes

And one with trembling hands clasps this cold head
And fans him with her moonlight wings, and cries;
Our love, our hope, our sorrow, is not dead

most other instruments are a surcharge don't-ya-know shed
beneath abandoned teeth— flats and naturals—
the lurid shine interprets the signatures, keys, sharps &
half-lit lonely weirdos of nature

the love that is truly a refuge for all living beings

Thermal Deformation of The Active Element Of A Periodic Mode
like the previous
moment of a ball of foam, but with regard
to the sounds that were, so to speak,
thrown away
through the process of making other pieces,
like the sprout from a rotten
seed, water music, impurity-induced
self-trapping of holes
and minority-ion percolation
like the erection of a eunuch,
like antennae,
and some were
like interruptions
of photoelectric
cells, living became something quite long that could be cut
up, stabilization of
stimulated extended-life emission like
thoughts of avarice, immorality,
wickedness, and hostility
in a bodhisattva who has attained tolerance,
photochemical, or
any other form of punctuation
the effect of the four
refractive indices
like the perception of
color in one blind
from birth like
the fun of games for one who wishes to die like
Blackbody radiation when I whispered it and cadences
became things

free of conceptualization, an empirical
luminescence discharge the
syllable passion spectra into the electric
fanning halide laser
a vast anomalous
reactive tangent
activity's
constructal
alms—
properties of properties dent
in welding this
weak collision, Aeons
of foci— tunable, coherent,
immeasurable

ROOF BOOKS

- ❏ Inman, P. **Red Shift**. 64p. $6.
- ❏ Lazer, Hank. **Doublespace**. 192 p. $12.
- ❏ Levy, Andrew. **Paper Head Last Lyrics**. 112 p. $11.95.
- ❏ Mac Low, Jackson. **Representative Works: 1938–1985**. 360p. $18.95 (cloth).
- ❏ Mac Low, Jackson. **Twenties**. 112p. $8.95.
- ❏ McMorris, Mark. **The Café at Light**. 112p. $12.95.
- ❏ Moriarty, Laura. **Rondeaux**. 107p. $8.
- ❏ Neilson, Melanie. **Civil Noir**. 96p. $8.95.
- ❏ Osman, Jena. **An Essay in Asterisks**. 112p. $12.95.
- ❏ Pearson, Ted. **Planetary Gear**. 72p. $8.95.
- ❏ Perelman, Bob. **Virtual Reality**. 80p. $9.95.
- ❏ Perelman, Bob. **The Future of Memory**. 120p. $14.95.
- ❏ Piombino, Nick, **The Boundary of Blur**. 128p. $13.95.
- ❏ Prize Budget for Boys, **The Spectacular Vernacular Revue**. 96p. $14.95.
- ❏ Raworth, Tom. **Clean & Will-Lit**. 106p. $10.95.
- ❏ Robinson, Kit. **Balance Sheet**. 112p. $11.95.
- ❏ Robinson, Kit. **Democracy Boulevard**. 104p. $9.95.
- ❏ Robinson, Kit. **Ice Cubes**. 96p. $6.
- ❏ Rosenfield, Kim. **Good Morning—MIDNIGHT—**. 112p. $10.95.
- ❏ Scalapino, Leslie. **Objects in the Terrifying Tense Longing from Taking Place**. 88p. $9.95.
- ❏ Seaton, Peter. **The Son Master**. 64p. $5.
- ❏ Sherry, James. **Popular Fiction**. 84p. $6.
- ❏ Silliman, Ron. **The New Sentence**. 200p. $10.
- ❏ Silliman, Ron. **N/O**. 112p. $10.95.
- ❏ Smith, Rod. **Music or Honesty**. 96p. $12.95
- ❏ Smith, Rod. **Protective Immediacy**. 96p. $9.95
- ❏ Stefans, Brian Kim. **Free Space Comix**. 96p. $9.95
- ❏ Tarkos, Christophe. **Ma Langue est Poétique—Selected Works**. 96p. $12.95.
- ❏ Templeton, Fiona. **Cells of Release**. 128p. with photographs. $13.95.
- ❏ Templeton, Fiona. **YOU—The City**. 150p. $11.95.
- ❏ Torres, Edwin. **The All-Union Day of the Shock Worker**. 112 p. $10.95.
- ❏ Tysh, Chris. **Cleavage**. 96p. $11.95.
- ❏ Ward, Diane. **Human Ceiling**. 80p. $8.95.
- ❏ Ward, Diane. **Relation**. 64p. $7.50.
- ❏ Watson, Craig. **Free Will**. 80p. $9.95.
- ❏ Watten, Barrett. **Progress**. 122p. $7.50.
- ❏ Weiner, Hannah. **We Speak Silent**. 76 p. $9.95
- ❏ Weiner, Hannah. **Page**. 136 p. $12.95
- ❏ Wellman, Mac. **Miniature**. 112 p. $12.95
- ❏ Wellman, Mac. **Strange Elegies**. 96 p. $12.95
- ❏ Wolsak, Lissa. **Pen Chants**. 80p. $9.95.
- ❏ Yasusada, Araki. **Doubled Flowering: From the Notebooks of Araki Yasusada**. 272p. $14.95.

ROOF BOOKS are published by
Segue Foundation • 300 Bowery • New York, NY 10012
Visit our website at **seguefoundation.com**

ROOF BOOKS are distributed by
SMALL PRESS DISTRIBUTION
1341 Seventh Avenue • Berkeley, CA. 94710-1403.
Phone orders: 800-869-7553
spdbooks.org